SandCastle 1

What Color is it?

Purple

Mary Elizabeth Salzmann

ABDO
Publishing Company

Published by SandCastle™, an imprint of ABDO Publishing Company, 4940 Viking Drive, Edina, Minnesota 55435.

Printed in the United States.

Cover and Interior Photo credits: Adobe, Díamar, Digital Stock, PhotoDisc
Library of Congress Cataloging-in-Publication Data

Salzmann, Mary Elizabeth, 1968–
    Purple / Mary Elizabeth Salzmann.
       p.   cm. -- (What color is it?)
    Summary: Simple text and photographs present a variety of purple
things, including a baseball uniform, inner tube, and swimsuit.
    ISBN 1-57765-160-X
    1. Colors--Juvenile literature. 2. Purple--Juvenile literature.
[1. Purple. 2. Color.] I. Title. II. Series: Salzmann, Mary
Elizabeth, 1968–   What color is it?
QC495.5.S28   1999
535.6--dc21
                                                             98-26684
                                                             CIP
                                                             AC

The SandCastle concept, content, and reading method have been reviewed and approved by a national advisory board including literacy specialists, librarians, elementary school teachers, early childhood education professionals, and parents.

Let Us Know

After reading the book, SandCastle would like you to tell us your stories about reading. What is your favorite page? Was there something hard that you needed help with? Share the ups and downs of learning to read. We want to hear from you! To get posted on the Abdo Publishing Company Web site, send us email at:

sandcastle@abdopub.com

About SandCastle™
Nonfiction books for the beginning reader

- Basic concepts of phonics are incorporated with integrated language methods of reading instruction. Most words are short, and phrases, letter sounds, and word sounds are repeated.

- Readability is determined by the number of words in each sentence, the number of characters in each word, and word lists based on curriculum frameworks.

- Full-color photography reinforces word meanings and concepts.

- "Words I Can Read" list at the end of each book teaches basic elements of grammar, helps the reader recognize the words in the text, and builds vocabulary.

- Reading levels are indicated by the number of flags on the castle.

Look for more SandCastle books in these three reading levels:

Level 1 (one flag)	**Level 2** (two flags)	**Level 3** (three flags)
Grades Pre-K to K 5 or fewer words per page	**Grades K to 1** 5 to 10 words per page	**Grades 1 to 2** 10 to 15 words per page

My shorts
are purple.

My uniform
is purple.

This curtain
is purple.

My hat is purple.

My inner tube
is purple.

My swimsuit
is purple.

My snow pants
are purple.

My shirt is purple.

My shirt is
purple, too.

Words I Can Read

Nouns

A **noun** is a person, place, or thing

curtain (KURT-uhn), p. 9

hat (HAT), p. 11

inner tube (IN-ur TOOB), p. 13

shirt (SHURT), pp. 19, 21

shorts (SHORTS), p. 5

snow pants (SNOH PANTS), p. 17

swimsuit (SWIM-soot), p. 15

uniform (YOO-nuh-form), p. 7

Verbs

A **verb** is an action or being word

are (AR), pp. 5, 17

is (IZ), pp. 7, 9, 11, 13, 15, 19, 21

Sight Words

curtain

shorts

hat

snow pants

inner tube

swimsuit

shirt

uniform